The Physical Sciences

ATOMS AND MOLECULES

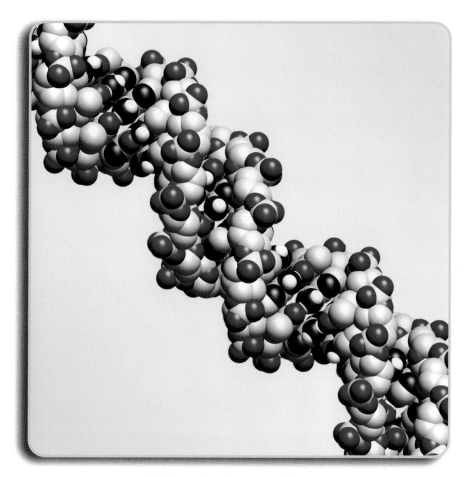

Nigel Saunders

WAYLAND

First published in 2007 by Wayland

Wayland
338 Euston Road
London NW1 3BH

Wayland
Level 17/207 Kent Street
Sydney, NSW 2000

Editor: Vicky Brooker

British Library Cataloguing in Publication Data
Saunders, N. (Nigel)
Atoms & molecules. - (The physical sciences)
1. Matter - Juvenile literature 2. Molecules - Juvenile literature
  I. Title 539.1

ISBN: 978 0 7502 5016 0

Printed in China

Wayland is a division of Hachette Children's Books.

Cover photograph: Richard Bradbury/Getty Images

Photo credits: p. 4: Philippe Plailly/Science Photo Library; p. 6: Rischgitz/Getty Images; p. 7: Chris Fairclough/CFWimages.com; p. 10: Bojan Tezak/istockphoto.com; p. 11: E.R.Degginger/Science Photo Library; p. 12: Andrew Lambert Photography/Science Photo Library; p. 14: Nick Schlax/istockphoto.com; p. 16: Darlyne A. Murawski/Getty Images; p. 17: Andrei Tchernov/istockphoto.com; p. 18: Jack Larmour/istockphoto.com; p. 19: iwka/istockphoto.com; p. 21: NOAA Photo Library/NOAA Central Library; (OAR/ERL/National Severe Storms Laboratory); p. 22: Edward Parker/EASI-Images//CFWimages.com; p. 23: Johan Eriksson/istockphoto.com; p. 24: Jake Norton/Aurora/Getty Images; p. 25: NASA; p. 26: Barbara Henry/istockphoto.com; p. 27: Andrew Lambert Photography/Science Photo Library; p. 28: Techstar; p. 29: Darla Hallmark/istockphoto.com; p. 30: Mark Scott/istockphoto.com; p. 33: Dawn Hudson/istockphoto.com; p. 34: Andrew Lambert Photography/Science Photo Library; p. 35: William Taufic/Corbis; p. 37: Simon Scoones/EASI-Images/CFWimages.com; p. 39 top: Chris Fairclough/CFWimages.com; p. 39 bottom: Stephen Martin/istockphoto.com; p. 40: Olly Hodgson/istockphoto.com; p. 41: Weldon Schloneger/istockphoto.com; p. 43: Alfred Benjamin/Science Photo Library; p. 44: Philips; p. 45: Sieto Verver

Contents

CHAPTER I

What are atoms and molecules?

Take a look around you. Every object you can see, including you and this book, is made from **matter**. Matter is anything that takes up space and weighs something on Earth. Some bits of matter are really big, like stars and planets, while other bits are much smaller. Just how small can matter get?

Atoms

Atoms are incredibly tiny. Three million gold atoms stacked on top of each other would only be one millimetre high. This is why we cannot see individual atoms. Atoms are the basic building blocks of matter. Everything is made from atoms and most atoms can join together in different ways to make all the different substances you see around you.

We cannot see individual atoms using an ordinary microscope, but they can be detected using a special one called a scanning tunnelling microscope. This is a photograph of a small pile of gold atoms (coloured yellow, red and brown) on a layer of carbon atoms (coloured green).

 PRINTING DOTS

Pictures from laser printers and inkjet printers are made from thousands of dots of ink. The more dots per inch, the better the picture, but the dots have to be really tiny. This is similar to matter in general: atoms are incredibly tiny and crammed together so closely that we cannot see them, only the matter itself.

INDIVISIBLE

The ancient Greek philosophers did a lot of thinking over two thousand years ago. They thought about matter and came up with an idea. They thought that it should be possible to divide an object over and over again, getting increasingly smaller pieces, but eventually you would get down to something really small. This really small piece of matter would be indivisible, which means it could not be split into anything smaller. The Greek word for indivisible is 'atomos', which is where we get the word 'atom'.

Inside atoms

Scientists have known for over a hundred years that atoms can be broken down into even smaller objects, called **sub-atomic particles**. At the centre of each atom there is a **nucleus**, which is made from two types of sub-atomic particles, called **protons** and **neutrons**. Clouds of sub-atomic particles called **electrons** are arranged around the nucleus at the edge of the atom.

Molecules

When atoms join together they make **molecules**. Some molecules are very simple and have only a few atoms each. Water molecules are like this. They each comprise one oxygen atom joined to two hydrogen atoms. Other molecules are very complex and have hundreds, thousands or sometimes millions of atoms each. The molecules that make up paper are like this and comprise thousands of carbon, oxygen and hydrogen atoms joined to make chains and branches.

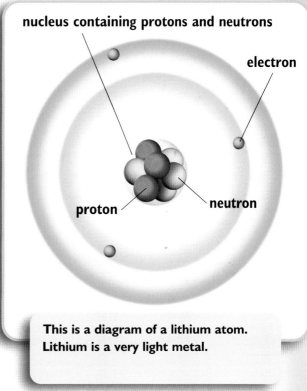

nucleus containing protons and neutrons

electron

proton

neutron

This is a diagram of a lithium atom. Lithium is a very light metal.

CHAPTER 2

The elements

There are over a hundred different **elements**. Gold, iron and chlorine are all elements, to name a few. An element is a substance that contains just one type of atom, and no two elements have the same type of atom. So, for example, oxygen atoms are different from gold atoms. Every substance that exists is made from one or more elements.

All alone or joined together

Molecules are made up of two or more atoms joined together. If the atoms in a molecule are all the same, you have an element. If there are two or more different atoms in a molecule, you have a **compound**. You will find out more about compounds in chapter three.

GREAT SCIENTISTS

John Dalton

John Dalton was an English scientist who developed the ancient Greek idea of atoms during the nineteenth century. His atomic theory included these ideas that have proved to be true: elements are made of tiny atoms; all the atoms of a given element are identical to each other; and the atoms of a given element are different from the atoms in other elements.

An illustration of John Dalton (1766-1844) in his laboratory.

Helium is an element whose atoms do not join with other atoms. It is less **dense** than air, so helium-filled party balloons float upwards.

The atoms of most elements join with each other to make molecules. Helium and neon are unusual elements. Their atoms do not join with any other atoms. They exist as single atoms, separated by empty space. Very few elements are like this. Only argon, krypton, xenon and radon also exist as single atoms, and even they can be forced to join with other atoms under extreme conditions.

Atomic number

Every atom consists of a central **nucleus** with **electrons** around it, so what is different about the atoms of different elements? The number of **protons** in the nucleus decides which element an atom belongs to. For example, every hydrogen atom has one proton, and every oxygen atom has eight protons. The number of protons in the nucleus is called the **atomic number**, and every element has a different atomic number.

 ANCIENT ELEMENTS

Nowadays we know that there are over a hundred different elements, but for thousands of years people believed that there were only four. These were earth, air, fire and water. Sometimes a fifth element, called ether, was included. Everything was believed to contain these elements in different proportions. However, we now know that earth and air are mixtures of elements and compounds, fire is heat energy and light energy, and water is a compound made from two elements.

The periodic table

Until 1750 only about sixteen **elements** were known. By the start of the nineteenth century this number had doubled, and by 1850 around sixty elements were known. Scientists were discovering more and more elements, and it was becoming increasingly difficult to make sense of it all. Some were very **reactive** and easily combined with other elements, while others only combined with other elements with difficulty. Scientists were keen to work out a way to organise the elements in a useful way.

Döbereiner's Triads

Different atoms have different **masses**. The actual mass of an atom in grams is difficult to measure, but atoms can be compared with each other instead. Hydrogen is the lightest atom and has an **atomic mass** of 1, while a really heavy atom like gold has an atomic mass of 197.

In 1829 a German chemist, Johann Döbereiner, noticed that some elements have similar properties. He put similar elements into 'triads', which were groups of three elements. Döbereiner discovered something interesting about the atomic mass of each element in a triad. The atomic mass of the middle element was the average of the atomic masses of the heaviest and lightest atoms. However, Döbereiner's triads were shortly to run into problems.

 GREAT SCIENTISTS

Newlands' Octaves

In 1864, an English chemist called John Newlands arranged the known elements in order of atomic mass. He found that each element had **properties** like the element eight places in front of it. Because there are eight musical notes in an octave, he called his arrangement the Law of Octaves. Unfortunately, some of his arrangements did not work because he did not leave gaps, as Mendeleev did. For example, he put iron in the same group as two **non-metals**, oxygen and sulfur. As a result, his table was not accepted by other scientists, who unkindly suggested that alphabetical order would be just as good.

Mendeleev's periodic table

Döbereiner's Triads, and later Newlands' Octaves (see box), were on the right track but suffered from a big problem. Chemists kept on discovering new elements, and neither system could cope with that. For example, one of Döbereiner's triads contained three metals: lithium, sodium and potassium. Then rubidium and caesium were discovered at the start of the 1860s. These have similar properties to lithium, sodium and potassium, so they belong in the triad too. But triads were only supposed to contain three elements, not five. In 1869, a Russian chemist called Dmitri Mendeleev published an arrangement that worked, called the periodic table. He put the elements in order of atomic mass, and he put similar elements into groups. But he also left gaps for undiscovered elements to fit into. These gaps meant that his table worked well, and could even be used to predict what the undiscovered elements would be like. His table was a great success, and all the gaps were eventually filled in as elements continued to be discovered.

> The modern periodic table is arranged in order of increasing **atomic number**. Similar elements are found in the columns, called groups. The metals are on the left and the non-metals are on the right. Elements 57-71 and 89-103 are so similar to each other, they are put in a separate block together at the bottom.

							H 1										He 2
Li 3	Be 4											B 5	C 6	N 7	O 8	F 9	Ne 10
Na 11	Mg 12											Al 13	Si 14	P 15	S 16	Cl 17	Ar 18
K 19	Ca 20	Sc 21	Ti 22	V 23	Cr 24	Mn 25	Fe 26	Co 27	Ni 28	Cu 29	Zn 30	Ga 31	Ge 32	As 33	Se 34	Br 35	Kr 36
Rb 37	Sr 38	Y 39	Zr 40	Nb 41	Mo 42	Tc 43	Ru 44	Rh 45	Pd 46	Ag 47	Cd 48	In 49	Sn 50	Sb 51	Te 52	I 53	Xe 54
Cs 55	Ba 56	57–71	Hf 72	Ta 73	W 74	Re 75	Os 76	Ir 77	Pt 78	Au 79	Hg 80	Tl 81	Pb 82	Bi 83	Po 84	At 85	Rn 86
Fr 87	Ra 88	89–103	Rf 104	Db 105	Sg 106	Bh 107	Hs 108	Mt 109	Ds 110	Rg 111							

La 57	Ce 58	Pr 59	Nd 60	Pm 61	Sm 62	Eu 63	Gd 64	Tb 65	Dy 66	Ho 67	Er 68	Tm 69	Yb 70	Lu 71
Ac 89	Th 90	Pa 91	U 92	Np 93	Pu 94	Am 95	Cm 96	Bk 97	Cf 98	Es 99	Fm 100	Md 101	No 102	Lr 103

☐ Metals   ☐ Metalloids   ☐ Non-metals

Metals

Copper, iron, gold and most other **elements** are metals. Metals have several **properties** in common. Apart from mercury, which is a liquid metal, all metals are solid at room temperature. They are all shiny, especially when freshly cut or scratched.

Conducting electricity and heat

Some of the **electrons** in metal atoms can leave the atoms and wander about from atom to atom. This is why metals are good **conductors** of electricity. When a piece of metal is connected in an electrical circuit, the electrons flow through the metal and carry their electric **charge** from one end to the other. Metals are also good conductors of heat because free electrons (the ones that can wander from one atom to another) can carry **thermal energy** from the hot end to the cold end.

AMAZING FACTS

Um...

If the name of an element ends in 'um' it belongs to a metal, with the exception of helium. Helium is actually a **non-metal**. This is because helium was first detected by studying sunlight and, as most elements are metals, it was imagined to be a metal. When helium was finally isolated by Sir William Ramsay in 1895, it was found to be a non-metal, but by then it was too late to change the name.

Mirrors are made by covering a sheet of aluminium or silver metal with glass.

Heavy metals

The atoms in metals are packed tightly together, so metals are usually very **dense**. This means that they are heavy for their size. Osmium is the densest metal – a teaspoon of it weighs 113 grams, or a quarter of a pound.

The atoms in a piece of metal are regularly arranged and have strong forces joining them together. This is why metals are usually strong, hard and tough, and why they are useful for making cars, buildings, bridges and ships. When a piece of metal is bent, layers of its atoms can slide over each other, so it does not shatter or snap unless a lot of force is used.

Lithium is the least dense metal. It is so light for its size, it floats on water. It also reacts with water, as you can see here.

THE MAGNETIC ELEMENTS

Some metals are magnetic. Magnets have many uses. You can find them in compasses and along the edge of refrigerator doors, while computer hard disks and credit cards use magnetic coatings to store information. Permanent magnets keep their magnetism and will attract iron, nickel and cobalt. These metals are magnetic because of the way their atoms and electrons are arranged.

Non-metals

Metals are placed on the left of the periodic table and **non-metals** on the right. Almost eighty per cent of the **elements** are metals and most of the rest are non-metals. Just one non-metal, bromine, is liquid at room temperature. Eleven non-metals are gases, like hydrogen and oxygen, and five are solid, like carbon and sulfur.

Just like metals, non-metal elements have several **properties** in common. They are usually dull when solid, rather than shiny. For example, sulfur, a non-metal element, is a dull, yellow solid. Solid non-metals are also brittle and easily shatter when hit with a hammer. Unlike metals, non-metals do not **conduct** electricity. This is because they do not have any free **electrons** to carry electric **charge** from place to place.

These are some of the seventeen non-metal elements. Clockwise from top left, they are sulfur, bromine, phosphorus, iodine and carbon.

Noble gases

Helium, neon, argon, krypton, xenon and radon belong to a group in the periodic table called the noble gases. They are called the noble gases because they do not react with other elements: they keep themselves apart, just as noblemen kept away from common people. The noble gases exist as single atoms while all the other non-metal elements exist as **molecules**.

(i) METALLOIDS

Eight elements have some of the properties of metals and some of the properties of non-metals. Elements like this are called metalloids. One of their important properties is that they are semi-conductors. This means that they do conduct electricity, but not as well as a metal. Silicon is a metalloid semi-conductor that is important for making computer chips.

Simple molecules

Apart from the noble gases, most of the non-metals exist as diatomic molecules. These are molecules that consist of two atoms joined together. Nitrogen and oxygen, the two main gases in the air you breathe, are always found as diatomic molecules. So is chlorine, the element used to kill harmful microbes in drinking water and swimming pools. There are only very weak forces attracting simple molecules like these towards each other, so they form gases.

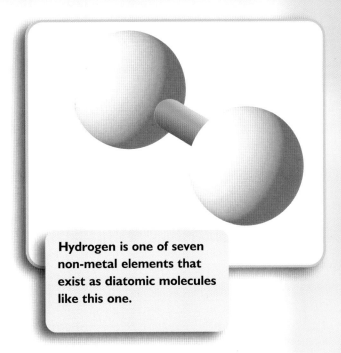

Hydrogen is one of seven non-metal elements that exist as diatomic molecules like this one.

Giant molecules

Carbon atoms form giant molecules which may contain many atoms. Diamond and graphite are the commonest forms of carbon. Each atom in diamond is joined to four others, making it solid and very hard, but brittle. A diamond is hard enough to cut glass, but will smash if you hit it with a hammer.

Graphite molecules are sheets of carbon atoms where each atom is joined to three others. The sheets can slide over each other, making graphite soft, slippery and useful for making pencil 'lead' (sticks of soft lead were used as pencils until 1564, when a deposit of very pure graphite was discovered in Borrowdale in England. Since then, the 'lead' in pencils has actually been graphite). Graphite conducts electricity, even though it is a non-metal, because it has electrons that are free to wander through it.

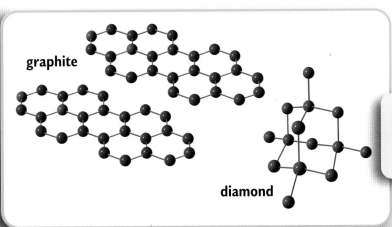

graphite

diamond

Diamond and graphite are both forms of carbon, but their molecules are very different.

CHAPTER 3

Compounds

Most of the substances around you are **compounds**. Compounds are substances made from two or more **elements** joined together by chemical **bonds**. Different compounds have different elements, and different numbers of atoms, in their **molecules**. But any particular compound has a constant proportion of the elements in its molecules. For example, ammonia is a compound made from nitrogen and hydrogen atoms. Every ammonia molecule contains one nitrogen atom and three hydrogen atoms, and no more or less than this.

Carbon dioxide

Carbon dioxide is the gas produced when fuels burn. Every carbon dioxide molecule is made from three atoms: one carbon atom and two oxygen atoms. Carbon dioxide is used in fire extinguishers and it puts the fizz in fizzy drinks.

> Carbon dioxide is a simple molecular compound that makes drinks fizzy.

 MADE FROM NON-METALS

When two **non-metal** atoms join together they make a type of bond called a covalent bond. These bonds form when the atoms get so close together that they can share two **electrons**, one from each atom. Covalent bonds are very strong and need a lot of energy to break, unlike the weak bonds between molecules. All the molecules described on these two pages contain covalent bonds.

AMAZING FACTS

Not like their elements

The **properties** of compounds are different from the properties of the elements they contain. Water molecules are made from hydrogen and oxygen atoms. Hydrogen and oxygen both form molecules that are gases at room temperature, yet water is a liquid. Similarly, carbon dioxide and natural gas both contain carbon atoms, but one puts out fires while the other is flammable. These differences exist because the atoms of each element are joined together in new ways in a compound.

Natural gas

Natural gas is used as a fuel for power stations and for cooking. It mostly contains a compound called methane. In the compound methane, every molecule consists of a carbon atom joined to four hydrogen atoms.

Water

Water is the most abundant compound on Earth. About 71 per cent of the Earth's surface is covered with it, and the oceans contain enough water for everyone on Earth to have their own drop three-quarters of a kilometre across. Every water molecule contains one oxygen atom joined to two hydrogen atoms.

These are just some of the many simple molecular compounds that exist.

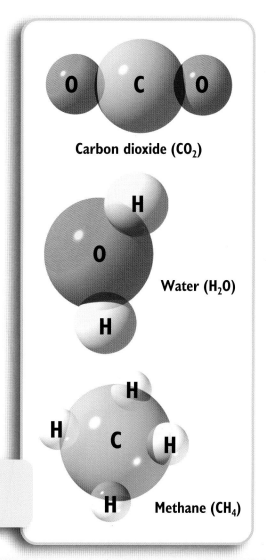

Carbon dioxide (CO_2)

Water (H_2O)

Methane (CH_4)

Giant molecular compounds

Simple molecular **compounds** contain only a few atoms, but giant molecular compounds contain hundreds, thousands or sometimes millions of atoms. A lot of your body is made from giant molecular compounds, including proteins and DNA. Some giant molecular compounds contain only a small number of different **elements**, while others contain several different elements joined together in complex ways.

Silica

Silicon and oxygen are the two most abundant elements in the Earth's crust. Just over a quarter of the **mass** of the crust is silicon and almost half is oxygen, so it's probably not surprising that their compound, silica, is a very common compound. You may have come across it on the beach, because it is the main compound in sand. It is also the main compound in glass.

Diatoms are tiny single-celled plants that make beautiful shells from silica, a giant molecular compound.

Silica is a giant **molecule**. Each molecule contains many millions of atoms, but there are always two oxygen atoms for every silicon atom. They are joined together to form a complex structure that makes silica hard and sharp.

Proteins

Proteins are complex molecules made from many atoms, including carbon, oxygen, nitrogen and hydrogen. All sorts of substances are proteins, including egg white, hair, nails, muscle and the mucus in your nose. Some proteins are soft and floppy, while others are hard and tough. It all depends on how the atoms are arranged in the molecule. Proteins are polymers, big molecules made from smaller molecules joined end to end.

PLASTICS

Plastics are polymers. They are made from thousands of smaller molecules called **monomers**. These join end to end to make a very long molecule. For example, ethene is a simple molecule containing two carbon atoms and four hydrogen atoms. Tens of thousands of ethene molecules join to form a single molecule of polythene. This is a plastic used for plastic bags and plastic bottles.

DNA

DNA stands for deoxyribonucleic acid. This is a long name for a long molecule, up to 7 cm long and made from small molecules joined end to end. The particular arrangement of these small molecules in a DNA molecule provides the **genetic code** for our **cells**. A gene is a section of DNA that has the code for a particular protein. For example, a certain gene might have the code that makes eyes blue, while another might have the code that makes eyes green. Although different species of animals and plants have genes in common, lots of genes vary between species.

DNA is a very complex molecule made from millions of atoms.

Ionic compounds

Ionic **compounds** are compounds of metals and **non-metals**. They don't contain **molecules**. Instead they are made from very many electrically **charged** particles called **ions**. Ions are made from atoms or groups of atoms. The ions are arranged in regular patterns, forming **crystals**. You are probably familiar with sodium chloride, or common table salt. It is an ionic compound and its crystals are tiny white cubes with flat sides. Other crystals have different colours and shapes.

Made from metals and non-metals

When a metal atom and a non-metal atom join together they make a type of **bond** called an ionic bond. These bonds form when the metal atom gives one or more **electrons** to the non-metal atom, forming electrically charged particles called ions. Metal ions are positively charged and non-metal ions are negatively charged. These oppositely charged ions attract each other strongly to make strong, ionic bonds, which need a lot of energy to break.

AMAZING FACTS

Gemstones

Precious stones like emerald and ruby are ionic compounds. Their crystals are coloured because of tiny amounts of certain metal atoms they contain. Emeralds are green and rubies are red because of tiny amounts of chromium. The crystals would be colourless without metal atoms like chromium, iron and manganese inside them.

Amethyst is purple because its crystals contain tiny amounts of manganese.

COLOURFUL COMPOUNDS

Many ionic compounds are white or colourless. These are the ones that contain metals from the first two columns of the periodic table, such as sodium, potassium and magnesium. If the compound contains a metal from the wide central block of the periodic table, such as copper or chromium, it is likely to be coloured.

Difficult to melt

Ionic compounds have high melting points and boiling points because a lot of energy is needed to separate the charged particles from each other. This means that ionic compounds are solid at room temperature. For example, sodium chloride melts at 804 °C (1479 °F) and magnesium oxide melts at 2800 °C (5072 °F).

Copper sulfate

Copper sulfate is a compound of copper, sulfur and oxygen. It forms deep blue crystals with slanting sides. The crystals are brittle and easily shatter when they are hit with a hammer.

Like many ionic compounds, copper sulfate easily dissolves in water. If the **solution** is heated, the water evaporates to leave blue crystals behind. But if these are heated strongly they eventually turn white. This is because the copper in the crystals are blue only when surrounded by water molecules.

These are blue copper sulfate crystals.

CHAPTER 4

The particle theory

Everything is made from atoms and **molecules**. If we understand the different ways these particles can be arranged and move, then many of the **properties** of the substances around us can be explained. The idea behind this is called the particle theory. It treats atoms and molecules as if they were incredibly tiny balls that are attracted towards each other if they get close enough. Particle theory uses this knowledge to explain how solids, liquids and gases behave.

States of matter

There are three familiar states of matter. These are solids, liquids and gases. For example, water is in the liquid state at room temperature, but water can become a solid if frozen (ice) and a gas if boiled (steam). In all three states the water particles are still water molecules, but they are arranged differently and move in different ways. These differences cause the different properties seen in ice, water and steam.

Solids

The particles in solids are very close together. They are arranged in orderly, regular ways. The particles in a solid are attracted to each other by forces called **bonds**. The bonds in solids are so strong that the particles are only able to vibrate and cannot move from place to place.

These diagrams show how the particles are arranged in solids, liquids and gases.

solid
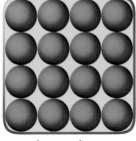
close, regular —
vibrate

liquid

close, random —
move around each other

gas
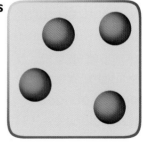
far apart, random —
move quickly in all directions

Liquids

The particles in liquids are very close together, just as they are in solids. However, they are randomly rather than regularly arranged. The particles in liquids can vibrate, just as they do in solids, but they can do something else as well. Some of the bonds between the particles in a liquid have been broken, so the particles can move around each other.

AMAZING FACTS

Absolute zero

The colder a solid gets, the more slowly its particles vibrate. The temperature at which they would not vibrate at all is called absolute zero. It is a very chilly -273.15 °C (-459.67 °F).

Gases

The particles in gases have managed to break all their bonds. This means that they are very far apart and can move very quickly in all directions. Just like the particles in a liquid, the particles in a gas are randomly arranged.

PLASMA

Most of the time we can happily talk about three states of matter but there is a fourth state, called plasma. Plasmas form when **electrons** are removed from particles of gas by heat or electricity, leaving hot electrically **charged** particles behind. Plasmas are found in the Sun, flames, fluorescent lighting, neon lights and plasma televisions.

The energy in lightning removes electrons from air particles, creating hot plasma as the lightning passes through the air.

Why fluids flow but solids don't

Take a glass and drop some ice cubes into it. The ice cubes rattle around in the bottom of the glass, and then you pour your drink until the glass is nearly full. You have just done a simple experiment to show that solids don't flow but liquids do. Gases flow, too, but it's harder to see because most gases are colourless. You can use particle theory to explain these **properties**.

Fluids and viscosity

Liquids and gases are fluids. Fluids can flow from place to place because their particles can move past each other. The easier it is for the particles to move past each other, the more easily the fluid can flow. The **viscosity** of a fluid tells you how easily it flows. Air and water are fluids with low viscosity. They flow easily. Treacle and oil are fluids with high viscosity. They flow with difficulty.

Crude oil is very viscous. Its **molecules** do not move past each other easily. When oil tankers are damaged it is very difficult to clean up the spilt oil because it is so thick and sticky.

! AMAZING FACTS

Superfluids

You have probably come across helium gas in party balloons, but it can be turned into a liquid by cooling. Normal, everyday fluids eventually stop spinning after being stirred, and they flow downwards when poured. Instead when helium gets below -271 °C (-455 °F), it becomes a superfluid. It keeps spinning after being stirred and even creeps up the sides of its container.

AMAZING FACTS

Non-Newtonian cornflour

If you stir water into cornflour you get a strange mixture that does some weird things. You can slowly scoop it into your hand and let it run through your fingers, but do this quickly and something else happens. The mixture seems to be rock solid. If you thump the mixture it is hard, yet you can slowly push your fingers into it. The mixture is an example of a 'non-Newtonian fluid'. It becomes more viscous the greater the force on it.

Solids

The particles in solids are attracted to each other by **bonds**. This stops them moving around each other or from place to place. Because of this, you cannot pour a solid or make it flow. Ice cubes rattle around in the bottom of a glass until they melt to form a liquid, which only then flows to cover the bottom of the glass.

Although lumps of solid will not flow, very fine pieces or powder can be poured. The pieces of solid are small enough to roll over each other, which is why you can pour sand from a bucket at the seaside. All the same, the particles in each grain of sand still cannot move around each other.

Grains of sand flow, but their individual atoms and molecules cannot.

Air pressure

Many people think that air doesn't weigh anything. After all, it is easy to bat a party balloon around the room. However, air contains **molecules** of nitrogen and oxygen, atoms of argon, and many other gases. Each individual atom and molecule has a very tiny **mass**. But there is more than 100 km of air above you, and the weight of all those atoms and molecules presses down on you on all sides. This is air pressure.

Standard atmospheric pressure is 101,325 newtons per square metre. This means that every square metre of you is pressed by a force of 101,325 newtons, equivalent to a mass of over ten tons! Luckily, you are pressed from all sides and your body pushes outwards to balance this, so you don't get squashed.

Different types of weather are accompanied by slightly lower or higher air pressure than average. Wet weather is generally linked to low pressure. Air rises in areas of low pressure. As the air rises, it cools and water vapour in it condenses to form clouds and rain. The mercury in a barometer falls if the air pressure is low, signalling wet weather. When the air pressure increases, the weather often improves and the mercury rises a little.

There are fewer atoms and molecules of air the higher you go so it is harder to breathe. Climbers have to use oxygen masks on very high mountains.

 GREAT EXPERIMENTS

Torricelli's experiment

Air pressure is measured using a device called a barometer. An Italian scientist, Evangelista Torricelli, invented the first barometer in 1643. He filled a long glass tube with mercury and turned it upside down in a dish of mercury. The mercury in the tube flowed out until the tube was filled to a height of 76 cm. The pressure of the air against the mercury in the dish balanced the weight of the mercury in the tube.

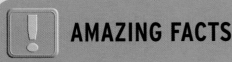
The *Apollo* spacecraft

The International Space Station in orbit around the Earth contains an atmosphere that is very similar to normal air. This was not the case when the *Apollo* space missions were sent to the Moon in the 1960s and 1970s. These spacecraft needed to be as light as possible to save fuel, so they contained an atmosphere of oxygen at lower than normal pressure. That way the walls of the spacecraft could be thinner and lighter.

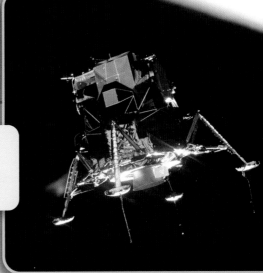

This is the Lunar Module in space during an *Apollo* mission to the Moon. The air inside was a third of normal air pressure.

The Magdeburg hemispheres

In 1650 Otto von Guericke, the mayor of Magdeburg in Germany, invented the first vacuum pump. A true vacuum contains no air at all and has zero air pressure. Von Guericke's pump was good enough to remove most of the air from containers, making a near vacuum inside with a very low pressure. In a series of experiments that drew crowds from far and wide, he used his pump to remove the air from two large copper cups with matching rims. When the air inside was removed, the air pressure outside the cups pushed them together. In fact, the cups were pushed together so forcefully that even teams of horses were not strong enough to pull them apart again. The cups could only be separated when air was let back in, making the air pressure the same inside and out.

Tyres

Have you ever tried to ride a bike with a flat tyre? It's not very easy. When air is pumped into a tyre, the atoms and molecules in the air rush around in all directions. They bump into each other and the walls of the tyre. When more air is squeezed into the tyre, gas particles hit the walls of the tyre more often, pushing against it and keeping the tyre inflated.

Diffusion

Have you ever smelled food cooking in the kitchen, even though you are in another room? If you have, the tempting smell has reached your nose because of a process called diffusion. Diffusion works because particles in liquids and gases can move around.

Diffusion in liquids

Some people have sugar in their tea or coffee. People usually stir their drink to dissolve the sugar, but leave it alone long enough and it will dissolve on its own. If you leave it even longer the sugar will eventually spread out through the whole drink because of diffusion. Diffusion happens because the dissolved sugar **molecules** are surrounded by water molecules, which can move and push the sugar molecules away.

Molecules from tea leaves dissolve in water and diffuse out of the tea bag into the rest of the cup.

GREAT SCIENTISTS

Graham's Law

Thomas Graham was a Scottish chemist who studied diffusion in gases. He discovered that the higher the **mass** of an atom or molecule the more slowly it diffused from place to place. For example, oxygen molecules have sixteen times the mass of hydrogen molecules. They diffuse four times more slowly than hydrogen molecules. Graham's Law can be used to compare gases to work out the masses of their molecules.

GREAT SCIENTISTS

Brownian motion

A Scottish biologist called Robert Brown discovered something unusual in 1827. While using a microscope to study pollen grains floating in water, he discovered that the pollen grains moved around randomly. This 'Brownian motion' happens because the grains are being constantly hit by water molecules from all directions, and so are pushed about randomly. Brownian motion also happens to smoke and dust particles in air or water because they get hit from all directions by air particles.

Diffusion in gases

Diffusion happens faster when a liquid or gas is warmed up. This is because the hotter the substance, the faster its particles move. Diffusion in gases happens much more quickly than diffusion in liquids because the particles in gases move more quickly than the particles in liquids. In fact, gas particles travel incredibly quickly. For example, oxygen molecules travel at 480 metres per second – about one and half times the speed of sound.

Unfortunately, an oxygen molecule doesn't get very far before hitting another oxygen molecule and bouncing off in another direction. Each one only travels 67 millionths of a millimetre before it hits another molecule, which it does every billionth of a second! So, smells do not reach your nose in a fraction of a second, but often take a few minutes.

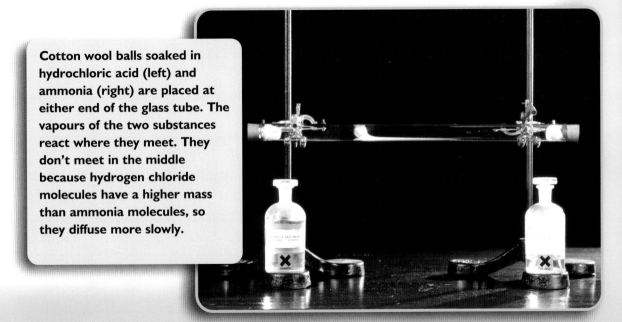

Cotton wool balls soaked in hydrochloric acid (left) and ammonia (right) are placed at either end of the glass tube. The vapours of the two substances react where they meet. They don't meet in the middle because hydrogen chloride molecules have a higher mass than ammonia molecules, so they diffuse more slowly.

Expansion and contraction

Most substances expand to fill more space when they are heated up and they contract to fill less space when they are cooled down. Expansion and contraction is all to do with atoms and **molecules**. When substances expand or contract, their atoms and molecules don't change size at all. It is the distance between them that gets bigger or smaller.

Solids

When a solid such as an iron bar warms up, its particles vibrate faster and move apart. This makes the solid expand to take up more room. This can be a problem for engineers. Steel railway lines expand during hot summer days and become longer. Gaps are needed between the rails, called expansion joints, to give the rails space to expand into. Without expansion joints, the railway lines would bend and buckle.

An expansion joint built into a bridge. The gaps between the vertical bars of metal will allow the bridge to expand in the summer heat without cracking.

 SHRINK-FITTING

Metal parts, such as cogs and shafts, can be joined without welding using shrink-fitting. The hole in the cog is slightly too small to fit the shaft at room temperature. But when the shaft is cooled down, it contracts and fits the hole. When the shaft warms up again, it expands into the hole in the cog and fits tightly.

Weird water

Water is very unusual. Most liquids contract when they are frozen, but water actually expands when it freezes. This is because the water molecules in ice arrange in a regular way that takes up more space. In very cold weather, the water in pipes can freeze. The ice pushes against the inside of the pipe until it splits. When the ice melts later, water spurts out of the damaged pipe.

Liquids

Liquids expand when they are heated because their particles move around more and so take up more room. This is useful for thermometers. The mercury or alcohol in the thermometer expands when it is warmed, so it rises up the tube. The hotter the liquid, the higher it rises.

Gases

Gases expand when they are heated because their particles move around faster and take up more room. Hot air balloons rely on this to stay in the air. The air inside the balloon is heated with a flame from a gas burner, making it expand. The air inside becomes less **dense** than the cold air outside because the particles are more spread out, and the balloon rises. The hot gas gradually cools and contracts again, so the burner must be used every so often to keep the balloon in the sky.

Hot air balloons rely on the expansion of air to stay in the sky.

Change of state

Substances change state when they are heated or cooled enough. For example, ice is solid water that melts to form liquid water when it is heated. If this is heated even more, the liquid water boils to form steam. This can be explained by looking at the forces between the particles.

Getting hotter

When a solid is heated to its melting point, its particles get enough energy to break some of the **bonds** holding them together. This allows the particles to move around each other, forming a liquid.

When a liquid is heated, its particles gain energy. Some of them have enough energy to break their bonds with other particles, so they escape from the liquid as a gas. This is called evaporation. When a liquid is heated to its boiling point, the liquid is evaporating as fast as it can, with many particles breaking their bonds and escaping.

Substances with high melting points and boiling points have strong bonds between their particles.

AMAZING FACTS

Sublimation

Some substances, like iodine, can change directly from a solid to a gas without becoming a liquid in between. This is called sublimation. Ice can sublime when the pressure around it is reduced. This is useful for freeze-drying coffee and other foods.

Solid carbon dioxide is called dry ice. This sublimes when warmed, creating a fog that is used for creepy effects in films.

Getting colder

When a gas is cooled, its particles lose energy. As it cools below its boiling point, bonds form between the particles and the gas condenses to form a liquid. Windows on a cold day have tiny droplets of water on them, called condensation. This forms because the cold glass cools water vapour from the air until it condenses.

When a liquid is cooled, its particles lose energy. As it cools below its freezing point, more bonds form between the particles and the liquid freezes to form a solid.

Cooling curves

The melting point and boiling point of a substance can be discovered using cooling curves. When a gas is cooled, its temperature goes down until it condenses. The temperature stays the same as the gas condenses, then goes down again once it is all liquid. The same thing happens as the liquid freezes.

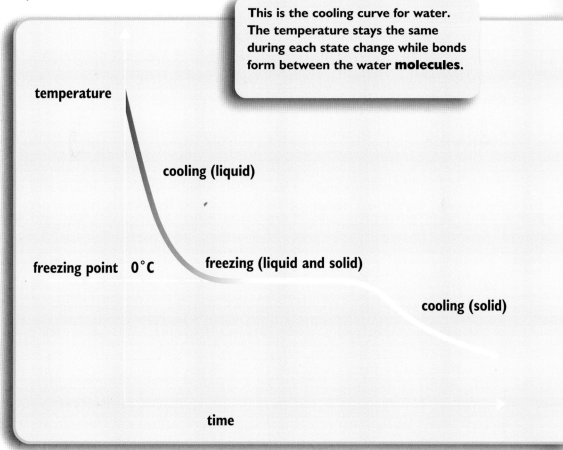

This is the cooling curve for water. The temperature stays the same during each state change while bonds form between the water **molecules.**

temperature

cooling (liquid)

freezing point   0°C

freezing (liquid and solid)

cooling (solid)

time

CHAPTER 5

Mixtures

Mixtures are very different to **compounds**. In compounds the different atoms are joined together in a fixed way, with **bonds** between them that only chemical reactions can separate. Mixtures, instead, are when different substances are thrown together and mixed up. The particles in a mixture are not joined together, which means that the different substances in a mixture are usually easily separated from each other.

Mixtures can contain individual atoms, **molecules** of **elements**, compounds, or any combination of these different types of particle. Mixtures do not have a fixed composition whereas compounds do. For example, a mixture of water and table salt can contain different amounts of salt, depending upon how much salt you stir into the water. But each water molecule always contains two hydrogen atoms and one oxygen atom, while the salt itself always contains equal numbers of sodium and chlorine **ions**.

Solutions

What happens when you mix sugar and water together? Unless you try to stir in a large mass of sugar into a small volume of water, eventually all the sugar **crystals** will disappear and you will be left with a clear, colourless sugar **solution**. The sugar is still there, however, because sugar crystals will be left behind if you evaporate the water.

 AIR - A BIG MIXTURE

The Earth's surface is covered by five thousand million million tons of air - plenty for everyone to breathe! It is a mixture of different elements and compounds. Just three elements account for 99.9 per cent of air: nitrogen molecules make up 78 per cent; oxygen molecules make up 21 per cent; and argon atoms make up 0.9 per cent. The remaining 0.1 per cent consists of many different gases, which are mainly compounds like carbon dioxide and water.

CONSERVATION OF MASS

If you were to mix 10 grams of salt into 100 grams of water you would find that the **mass** of the solution would be 110 grams. The salt particles are still there, just separated and spread through the water. This is called conservation of mass, and it applies to any solute, solvent and solution.

When a **solute** like sugar dissolves in a **solvent** like water, its crystals become smaller and smaller until they can no longer be seen. The sugar molecules can only vibrate because they are in the solid state, but the water molecules can move around because they are in the liquid state. Water molecules surround individual sugar molecules and carry them away from the crystals. Eventually all the sugar molecules become spread out through the water and we say that the sugar has dissolved.

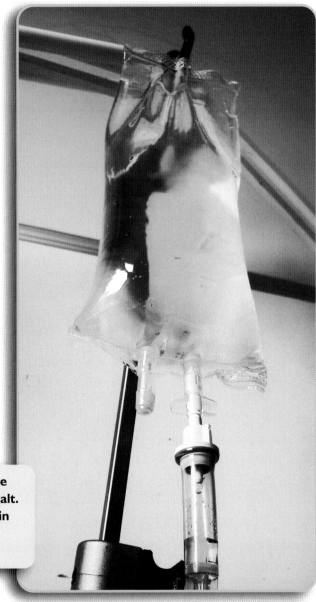

Intravenous drips like this one are solutions of glucose and salt. They replace the body fluids in ill patients.

Separating solutions

There are many ways to separate the different substances in a mixture. Sometimes it happens by accident. For example, if you almost finish a glass of cola or fruit juice and leave the glass to one side, the water from the drink evaporates leaving a sticky stain behind. Evaporation of the **solvent** is a simple way to get the **solute** on its own. But what if you want to get the solvent on its own, and you have a mixture of different liquids or a mixture of different solutes?

Distillation

Distillation is used to separate the solvent in a **solution** from the solute. The solution is heated so that the solvent boils. Its vapours are led away in pipes, then cooled and condensed back to a liquid. Distillation is useful for making drinking water out of seawater.

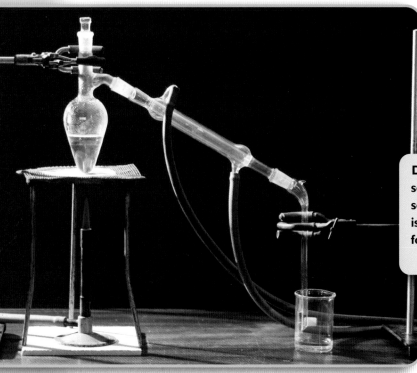

Distillation is used to separate the solvent in a solution. Equipment like this is often used in laboratories for distillation.

Fractional distillation is used to separate mixtures of two or more liquids, such as gasoline and diesel from crude oil. The liquid with the lowest boiling point turns into a gas first. Its vapours are led away and condensed back to a liquid. The process works because the substances have different boiling points, as the **bonds** between the **molecules** in different substances have different strengths. Alcohol has a lower boiling point than water, so they can also be separated using fractional distillation. This is used for making liquor like whisky.

Chromatography

Inks, and many other coloured liquids, are actually mixtures of different solutes. Chromatography can separate the different coloured solutes in these mixtures. A small volume of the coloured liquid is added to the bottom of a piece of filter paper. This is then placed upright in a tank containing a shallow depth of a solvent such as water. The solvent soaks up through the paper, taking the different coloured solutes with it. The different coloured substances move upwards at different speeds. After a while, some have reached the top while others have stayed near the bottom.

Chromatography is useful to investigate the different coloured substances in leaves. Although most leaves appear green because of the chlorophyll they contain, they also contain yellow and orange substances. Forensic scientists can use chromatography to see if there is a match between the ink used to forge a signature and the ink in a pen taken from a suspect.

Chromatography is used to separate different coloured solutes from each other.

Insoluble substances

There is a limit to how much **solute** can dissolve in a **solvent**. For example, if you keep adding more and more salt to water, eventually you find that no more salt dissolves. The **solution** has become **saturated** with salt. If you then add even more salt, it just sinks to form a **sediment**. More salt will dissolve if the water is warmed up because the **solubility** of most solids increases as the temperature increases. However, some substances don't dissolve at all. Chalk and metals are **insoluble**.

Filtration

Filtration separates an insoluble substance from a liquid or gas. It works because the filter paper has tiny holes that are only big enough to let the liquid or gas **molecules** through. The substance that goes through the paper is called the filtrate, and the solid that stays behind is called the residue. Filtration is used in water treatment plants as part of the process to make water safe for drinking.

Try another solvent

Substances that will not dissolve in water may dissolve in other solvents. Nail polish does not dissolve in water because its molecules cannot form **bonds** with the water molecules. But it will dissolve in a liquid called propanone, or acetone, which is the main ingredient of nail polish remover. Similarly, household gloss paint does not dissolve in water, so an oil-based solvent called paint thinner is often used to clean the brushes.

 AMAZING FACTS

Desalinating water

About 97 per cent of the Earth's water is seawater and so not suitable for drinking because of its salt. Rivers contain just a millionth of the world's water. Desalination plants can provide fresh water from seawater. The seawater is squeezed through a filter with microscopic holes. These are big enough to let water molecules through, but too small for salt and other dissolved particles.

WHY BEACHES DON'T DISSOLVE

Why are there sandy beaches? Salt dissolves in water, which is why the sea is salty, but sand cannot dissolve in water. The silica molecules in sand cannot form chemical bonds with water.

Sand is insoluble, so the sea can roll over a sandy beach, but it cannot dissolve the sand.

When your clothes get dirty, greasy stains are difficult to remove because the molecules in the stain do not dissolve in water. You can use a detergent to help dissolve them, but some clothes are damaged in water. Instead, the clothes are cleaned at a dry cleaning shop. It is called 'dry' cleaning because instead of using water, they clean using solvents such as tetrachloroethene.

AMAZING FACTS

Dissolving glass

The silica molecules in sand can form some chemical bonds with sodium hydroxide solution, a strong **alkali**. When it forms these bonds, small amounts of the sand will dissolve. Glass is made from molten sand that is cooled quickly to form a transparent solid. If you store sodium hydroxide solution in glass containers with glass stoppers, the stoppers eventually become stuck.

CHAPTER 6

Rocks

The Earth is sometimes described as a rocky planet because, unlike gas giants like Jupiter, the Earth has a solid, rocky crust. You might think that a rock is just a rock, but there are lots of different types. Rocks contain grains, each made from a **compound** called a mineral, and rocks are often mixtures of different minerals.

Weathering

Rocks do not stay the same forever. They are broken down, or weathered, by different processes. Rocks are lashed by wind and rain, which separate their grains and break them down. Acids in rain and soil react with some of the minerals, causing the rocks to crumble. Plants and burrowing animals also play a part in weathering. Plant roots grow down into tiny cracks and, as they grow, they get fatter and push the cracks open. Ice does a similar job because when water freezes in cracks, the ice expands and forces the cracks open.

Erosion and transport

Broken pieces of weathered rock tumble downwards and may pile up at the bottom of rock faces and cliffs. These eroded pieces may be washed away by rivers, which transport them towards the sea. When they get there, they may eventually become new rocks.

AMAZING FACTS

Onion skin weathering

Rocks in deserts can be broken down by onion skin weathering. This happens because the outer layers of the rock expand in the hot daytime, then cool down and contract in the cold night. Over time, this causes cracks and the outer layers fall off.

Sedimentary rocks

Limestone and shale are examples of sedimentary rocks, a type of rock formed from the remains of other rocks. When a river reaches the sea, it slows down and drops its load of eroded rock pieces. These sink to the sea bed and form layers called **sediments**. Over many years, the weight of the sediments on top presses down on the sediments below. This squeezes the water out and dissolved salts form **crystals** between the pieces of rock. They gradually cement or join the pieces together to form new, sedimentary rock.

These are limestone cliffs at Beachy Head in England. The sea crashes against the cliffs, gradually weathering them and causing chunks of limestone to fall onto the beach below.

! AMAZING FACTS

Fossils

If a dead animal or plant gets trapped in sediments, it gets covered and does not decay properly. Instead, over many years its **molecules** are replaced by minerals. Eventually a fossil forms. Usually only the hard parts like bones are fossilised. Fossils can be used to date rocks. For example, if a creature lived 100 million years ago, this must be the age of the rock its fossil is found in.

Fossilised remains of animals and plants may be found in sedimentary rocks.

Metamorphic and igneous rocks

The surface of the Earth is being changed all the time. Large movements of the crust can bury rocks deep underground. When this happens, the rocks can be changed into new rocks.

GREAT SCIENTISTS

Alfred Wegener's continental drift theory

Alfred Wegener was a German scientist. In 1912, he put forward the idea that the continents used to be one huge land mass that split apart and, over millions of years, the different pieces moved to form the world we see today in maps. It took a long time for his idea to be accepted because it was difficult to see how the continents could move. We now know that the continents are huge pieces of crust called tectonic plates. These float on the mantle, a layer of rock inside the Earth that is solid but can flow slowly like a **viscous** liquid.

Metamorphic rocks

When rocks are buried deep underground they are compressed, or squashed. They heat up but they do not always melt. Instead, the pressure and heat changes the structure of the **crystal** grains in the rocks. The atoms or **molecules** in the minerals are pushed closer together into new arrangements, creating a new crystal structure. For example, limestone becomes marble and shale becomes slate.

Slate is a metamorphic rock that is easily split into flat sheets. It is useful for making roofs.

Igneous rocks

When rocks are buried deep underground they may become hot enough to melt. Molten rock, called magma, forms. When magma cools and solidifies it forms new rocks, called igneous rocks. Crystals grow as the magma solidifies. When the magma becomes completely solid, the crystals lock together, rather like pieces of a jigsaw puzzle.

If the magma cools slowly underground, the crystals grow to a large size and we get an intrusive igneous rock. Granite is like this. Magma cools quickly if it escapes from a volcano onto the land or sea bed. Only small crystals form and we get an extrusive igneous rock such as basalt. Sometimes magma cools so quickly that no crystals form, just a sort of natural glass. Obsidian is a black, glassy rock formed this way.

 Granite is a hard, tough rock. It is used in public buildings where its coloured crystals give an attractive finish.

! AMAZING FACTS

Are the oceans getting saltier?

The oceans are salty because rivers carry dissolved salts from weathered rock to them. You might imagine that the oceans are getting more salty all the time, but scientists believe that they have stayed much the same for over a billion years. This is because continental drift pushes some parts of the ocean floor underneath the land, taking salty water with it. This is replaced when water vapour in the air condenses, falls as rain and flows down to the ocean in rivers.

CHAPTER 7

Atoms and molecules in the future

We continue to discover more and more about the world of atoms and **molecules**. It is possible to make new molecules and even new atoms, substances that have never existed before.

Strange atoms

Uranium is the naturally occurring **element** with the heaviest atoms. Its atoms have an **atomic number** of 92, and any heavier atoms must be made artificially. One way to do this is to set off an atomic bomb and analyse its **fallout**. Einsteinium, atomic number 99, was discovered this way. However, new atoms are usually made by bombarding atoms with other atoms or pieces of atoms in machines called particle accelerators. Over twenty new elements have been discovered this way, including one with an atomic number of 116. There's just one problem: these new atoms are **radioactive** and break down again in fractions of a second so it is hard to study them.

AMAZING FACTS

How many natural elements?

It is often said that there are 92 natural elements but there are fewer than this. Some atoms are radioactive and quickly fall apart. This means that the atoms of some elements only exist for a very short time and must be made artificially. Technetium and promethium are like this. Technetium was the first element to be produced artificially and is even named after the Greek word for 'artificial'.

Liquid crystals

Liquid **crystals** are strange molecules that are a bit like a liquid and a bit like a solid. Like a liquid, the crystals are able to move around each other. But like a solid, the crystals can line up in regular arrangements. When they are lined up, liquid crystals reflect light in a certain way, and this is the basis of liquid crystal displays, or LCDs.

By controlling electricity flowing through different parts of the display, the liquid crystals can be made to line up or not, showing clear or dark areas in the screen. All sorts of portable electronic devices use LCDs, including telephones and calculators, because very little battery power is needed to get them to work.

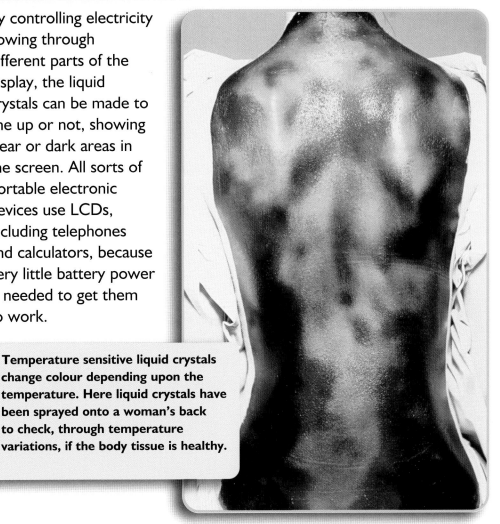

Temperature sensitive liquid crystals change colour depending upon the temperature. Here liquid crystals have been sprayed onto a woman's back to check, through temperature variations, if the body tissue is healthy.

 AMAZING FACTS

Liquid crystal thermometers

Thermometers often use mercury or alcohol in a glass tube, or an electronic device, to show the temperature. Others use liquid crystals to show the temperature. Liquid crystals are very close to being a real liquid, so they are sensitive to temperature. Liquid crystal thermometers are plastic strips with numbers in boxes. Different boxes change colour at different temperatures. This works because each box contains slightly different liquid crystals, which melt at different temperatures.

Atomic machines

You may be familiar with downloading computer games and software updates from the Internet, but what if you could download a new mobile phone? It sounds crazy but it may become possible very soon. Welcome to the world of nanotechnology and designer **molecules**.

Microprocessors

Many modern devices contain **microprocessors**, including computers, mobile phones, cars and even washing machines. Often called computer chips, microprocessors are built out of silicon and a few other **elements** such as arsenic and boron. They can contain over a hundred million electronic components crammed together. Modern chips have components that are so small that they are only a few hundred atoms wide. But scientists are aiming to go even smaller. They have produced wires just ten atoms thick.

A microprocessor is so small that it can be held in the jaws of an ant.

AMAZING FACTS

Writing with atoms

Researchers did something incredible in 1990. They used a machine called a scanning tunnelling microscope to move 35 xenon atoms, one at a time, onto a nickel **crystal**. When they had finished, the atoms spelled out the initials of their company in letters so tiny they could only be seen using an electron microscope – an ordinary microscope wasn't good enough. This scale of working is called nanotechnology because a nanometre is a millionth of a millimetre, about the size of a few atoms.

AMAXING FACTS

Print your own mobile phone

Ordinary printers use ink in two dimensions on paper, but three-dimensional printers use lasers to make solid objects such as shoes, layer by layer. The laser is programmed to heat up powdered nylon in just the right places until it joins together. Eventually it will be possible to use metals and other materials. The process is still too expensive for everyday use, but one day it may become cheap enough for us to download designs, and then print our own mobile phones and other equipment.

Nanotechnology

Nanotechnology involves incredibly tiny particles, often only a few atoms in size, called nanoparticles. Sunblock creams may contain titanium dioxide or zinc oxide nanoparticles about thirty millionths of a millimetre across. This is small enough to make the sunblock transparent but still able to stop harmful **ultraviolet** light from the Sun reaching the skin. Some nanotechnology involves truly tiny machines.

Researchers have built pumps, motors and many other devices that are so small we need a microscope to see them. We already have tiny 'labs' on chips, where all the parts needed to analyse chemicals are on a computer chip. One day, tiny 'nanobots' might patrol our bodies, repairing damaged cells.

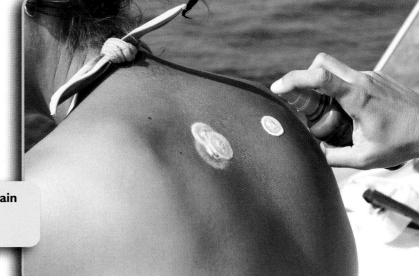

Sunblock creams may contain microscopic nanoparticles.

Glossary

alkali a substance with a pH greater than 7 which can react with acids.

atomic mass the mass of an atom compared to other atoms.

atomic number the number of protons in the nucleus of an atom.

bonds forces attracting atoms or molecules towards each other.

cells the small parts that living things are made from.

charge a unit of electricity – charges can be positive or negative.

compound a substance made of two or more elements joined together.

conductors substances that allow heat or electricity to pass through them.

crystals solids where the particles are regularly arranged, giving flat sides.

dense substances that are very dense are very heavy for their size.

electrons negatively charged sub-atomic particles in an atom.

elements substances that cannot be made simpler using chemical reactions.

fallout the substances produced in an explosion, especially from an atomic bomb.

genetic code information in our cells that is inherited from our parents.

insoluble not able to dissolve in a particular solvent.

ions charged particles made from atoms or groups of atoms.

mass how much matter an object contains, usually measured in kilograms or grams.

matter anything that takes up space and would weigh something on Earth.

microprocessor a computer processor contained on an integrated-circuit chip. Sometimes called a computer chip.

molecules particles made from two or more atoms joined together – they can be elements or compounds.

monomers small molecules that can join end to end.

neutrons neutral sub-atomic particles found in the nucleus of an atom.

non-metals substances that are not shiny and do not conduct heat or electricity well.

nucleus central part of an atom.

properties how a substance behaves and appears. Chemical properties describe how it reacts with other substances, and physical properties describe things like state and colour.

protons positively charged sub-atomic particles in the nucleus of an atom.

radioactive able to give off invisible radiation.

reactive able to react with another substance easily.

saturated a solution in which no more solute will dissolve.

sediment layer of undissolved solid.

solubility a measure of how much solute can dissolve.

solute the substance that dissolves in a solvent.

solution the mixture formed when a solute dissolves in a solvent.

solvent liquid or gas in which a solute dissolves.

sub-atomic particles particles smaller than an atom.

thermal energy heat energy.

ultraviolet invisible light just past the blue end of the spectrum.

viscosity a measure of how easily a fluid flows. The more viscous a fluid is, the thicker it is.

Further information

Books

Horrible Science: Chemical Chaos, Nick Arnold. Scholastic Hippo, 1997.

Material Matters: Mixtures, Compounds and Solutions, Carol Baldwin. Raintree Freestyle, 2005.

Science Files: Rocks and Minerals, Steve Parker. Heinemann Library, 2002.

Wow Science Series: Chemistry – Flames Are Stored Sunlight, Bryson Gore. Franklin Watts Ltd, 2005.

Websites

WebElements
http://www.webelements.com
An interactive periodic table crammed with information and photographs.

Skoool.co.uk
http://kent.skoool.co.uk
Choose a topic, learn all about it and then take a test or see a simulation. Choose 'key stage 3' then 'Chemistry' to find out about atoms and molecules.

BBC Science
http://www.bbc.co.uk/science
Quizzes, news, information and games about all areas of science.

BBC Bitesize
http://www.bbc.co.uk/schools/ks3bitesize/science/chemistry
Lots of information about atoms, molecules and aspects of chemistry.

Index